TOTALLY RANDOM

QUESTIONS

VOLUME **2**

101 Odd and Awesome Q&As

Melina Gerosa Bellows

NEW YORK

Contents

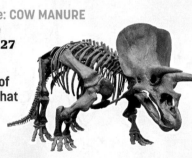

Which mammal has the heaviest brain on Earth?

a. the elephant

b. the sperm whale

c. the hippopotamus

ANSWER: b

the sperm whale

THE SPERM WHALE HAS THE LARGEST-KNOWN BRAIN OF ANY ANIMAL, LIVING OR EXTINCT. Its brain weighs as much as **20 pounds (9 kg)—5 times heavier than a human's!** The male sperm whale's head alone takes up about one-third of its total body length. This gigantic sea creature is also the **largest-toothed predator on the planet.** Sperm whales are found in all oceans, from the equator to the frigid waters of the Arctic and Antarctic.

Instant Genius

Sperm whales live about 70 years. Some may live longer.

True or False: **Birds** *sweat.*

#2

ANSWER: **False**

WHEN BIRDS ARE HOT, THEY HAVE SEVERAL WAYS THEY CAN COOL OFF. Some birds use their bills to control their body temperature by **increasing or decreasing blood flow into the beak.** Birds with larger bills, such as the toucan, which lives in a tropical rain forest, tend to live in warmer climates. Some species, such as nighthawks, will **open their mouths and "flutter" their neck muscles to release heat.** Other birds use their wings to stay cool. Great blue herons open their wings to move cooling air across their torsos, and mother herons have been observed **spreading their wings like an umbrella** to shade their chicks.

Nighthawk

Instant Genius

Birds don't have sweat glands.

Mother heron shading her chicks

12

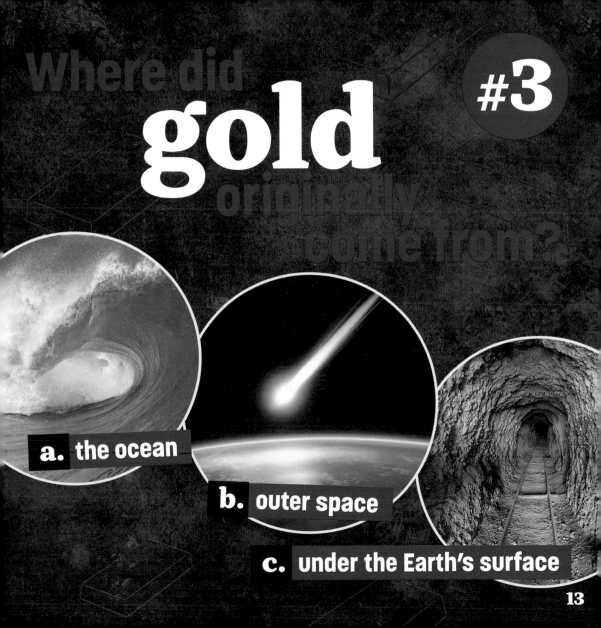

Where did **gold** originally come from?

#3

a. the ocean

b. outer space

c. under the Earth's surface

ANSWER: **b** **outer space**

WE GET GOLD BY MINING IT FROM THE GROUND. But scientists believe that gold was first created in the stars and came to Earth when **meteorites hit the planet 200 million years ago.** Gold is a heavy, shiny metal that is also a chemical element. It is rare and valuable, and it has been **used for thousands of years as a form of money and as jewelry,** among other things. Because it is soft, gold is easier to mold than other metals. We still use gold for jewelry, but it is also used in new technologies such as **medical devices and computers.**

NOW YOU KNOW!
Unlike many other metals, gold doesn't wear away or rust. Gold jewelry and other items created by ancient civilizations have been found in perfect condition.

An ancient Inca carving of a face, made of all gold

What is the official sport of the U.S. state of Alaska?

#4

a. skiing

b. dog mushing

c. ice skating

Iditarod Trail Sled Dog Race

ANSWER: b

dog mushing

THE INDIGENOUS PEOPLES OF ALASKA AND THE ARCTIC USED DOGS TO PULL SLEDS FOR THOUSANDS OF YEARS. Dogs and sleds are sometimes still used as a form of transportation, usually to deliver supplies such as wood, milk, or even mail to very rural and other hard-to-reach places. But today dogs and sleds go together mainly in a sport called mushing, which **became Alaska's official state sport in the early 1970s.** Two of the most famous dog sled races in the world are the **Iditarod Trail Sled Dog Race** and **Yukon Quest in Alaska.** Fans of mushing are hoping to have it included as a sport in future Winter Olympics.

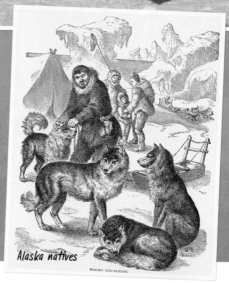

Alaska natives

ESKIMO DOG-SLEDGE.

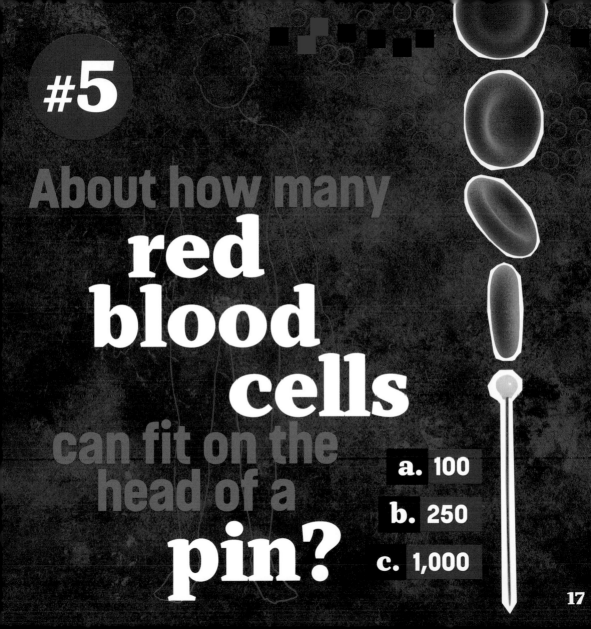

#5

About how many **red blood cells** can fit on the head of a **pin?**

a. 100

b. 250

c. 1,000

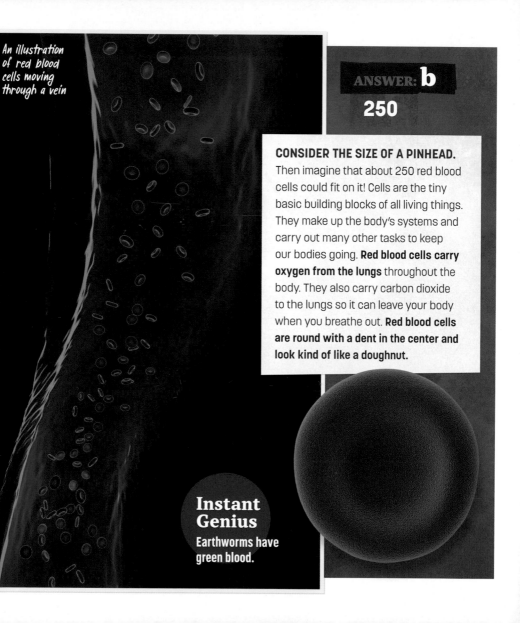

An illustration of red blood cells moving through a vein

CONSIDER THE SIZE OF A PINHEAD. Then imagine that about 250 red blood cells could fit on it! Cells are the tiny basic building blocks of all living things. They make up the body's systems and carry out many other tasks to keep our bodies going. **Red blood cells carry oxygen from the lungs** throughout the body. They also carry carbon dioxide to the lungs so it can leave your body when you breathe out. **Red blood cells are round with a dent in the center and look kind of like a doughnut.**

Instant Genius
Earthworms have green blood.

Warthogs
have
warts.

#6

ANSWER: **False**

WARTHOGS HAVE LARGE, FLAT HEADS WITH TWO PAIRS OF TUSKS THAT CURVE UPWARD. They also have thick, fleshy bumps on their faces. But these bumps are not warts. **Warts are small, hard, rough growths** (usually on the hands or feet) caused by a virus. **The bumps on a warthog are extra skin to protect its face.** All warthogs have them: Females have two small bumps beneath their eyes, while males have four—two large ones beneath the eyes and two smaller ones just above the mouth.

Instant Genius

A warthog's tusks help it defend itself against predators such as lions and leopards.

#7

What is a bat's preferred food?

Dinnertime!

a. insects   b. spiders   c. lizards

White-throated round-eared bat eating a katydid

Instant Genius

Blood is the only food a vampire bat eats.

ANSWER: a **insects**

BATS ARE NOCTURNAL, SO NIGHTTIME IS WHEN THEY LOOK FOR FOOD. Depending on the species, bats will eat fruit, nectar, and pollen, but insects are what they prefer. **A single bat can eat thousands of insects a night,** and this insect-rich diet has benefits for farmers: Because bats consume so many bugs, **they keep the pest population under control,** which protects crops. Bats locate their meals using echolocation, which means **they send out sound waves that bounce back when they hit an object.** Once a bat locates an insect, it will trap it using its wing or tail. Then, the bat reaches for the insect and puts it in its mouth.

NOW YOU KNOW!

Vampire bats don't suck on the blood of their prey. Instead, they make tiny cuts with their teeth, then lick it up.

Vampire bat

True or False:

Hurricanes

are also called typhoons or cyclones.

#8

23

HURRICANES ARE ALSO CALLED CYCLONES OR TYPHOONS, DEPENDING ON WHERE THEY OCCUR. Storms that form over the North Atlantic Ocean and the central and eastern North Pacific Ocean are called hurricanes. Storms that form over the South Pacific and Indian Oceans are called tropical cyclones. And storms that form over the northwestern Pacific Ocean are called typhoons. No matter what they're called, though, these are **large, powerful rotating storms with high-speed winds that form over warm waters in tropical areas**—and they are capable of deadly destruction. To be considered a hurricane, cyclone, or typhoon, **a tropical storm must have winds of at least 74 miles an hour (119 kmh).**

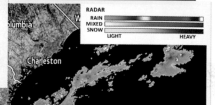

RADAR
RAIN
MIXED
SNOW
LIGHT   HEAVY

Columbia

Charleston

Baton Rouge

New Orleans

Tallahassee

Jacksonville

Houston

Daytona Beach

Counterclockwise

Tampa

Fort Myers

Miami

Nassau

Key West

intellicast

Instant Genius

Storms are named after people so that the storms can be identified quickly.

How long can a cockroach live without its head?

a. about seven minutes

b. about seven hours

c. about one week

about one week

Instant Genius
The life span of an adult American cockroach (*with its head!*) is about one year.

COCKROACHES CAN BE FOUND ALMOST ANYWHERE, INCLUDING PEOPLE'S HOMES . . . *ICK!* They are born survivors that can even live for about a week without their heads. How is that possible? **A cockroach won't bleed to death** if it loses its noggin. Unlike a human, whose blood flows through arteries and veins, a cockroach's blood sloshes around its tissues, so **blood in a headless roach would just clot at the neck.** A headless cockroach wouldn't suffocate, either: These sturdy insects get oxygen through small holes in their bodies called spiracles, so **they don't need noses or mouths to breathe.**

NOW YOU KNOW!
A headless cockroach would eventually die from hunger and thirst. Without a mouth, it wouldn't be able to eat or drink.

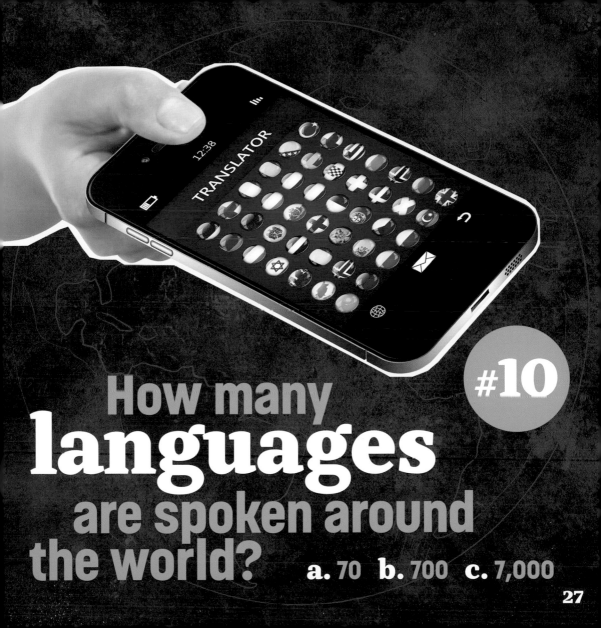

How many languages are spoken around the world?

#10

a. 70   b. 700   c. 7,000

Hello = 你好 nǐ hǎo

ANSWER: C **7,000**

APPROXIMATELY 7,000 DIFFERENT LANGUAGES ARE SPOKEN AROUND THE WORLD. But almost half of the people in the world mainly speak one of only 10 languages. More than 900 million people speak Chinese as their first, or native, language. **Native Chinese is the most spoken language in the world. It's followed by Spanish,** with about 460 million native speakers. Spanish is the main language in Spain and most of Central and South America. There are 379 million native English speakers, making **English the third most spoken native language.** More than 753 million additional people speak English as a second language because **English is the most common language used in business and travel.**

Instant Genius

Languages can go extinct. Today there are 44 languages that have only one or two speakers.

Who is more often color-blind?

a. Men are.

b. Women are.

c. It's a tie.

ANSWER: a

Men are.

NINETY-FIVE PERCENT OF PEOPLE WHO ARE COLOR-BLIND ARE MEN. But being color-blind doesn't mean you can't see *any* color—it means **you have trouble telling the difference between greens and reds,** and sometimes blues. **(In severe cases, everything looks gray.)** In the eye, the retina has two types of cells that detect light: rods and cones. Rod cells detect only light and dark. Cone cells detect color. In humans there are three types of cones that register color: red, green, and blue. **In people who are color-blind, the cone cells aren't functioning properly.**

Instant Genius

Dogs are color-blind, but they can detect yellow, blue, and gray.

NOW YOU KNOW!

Color blindness is genetic, which means that it is passed from parents to their children.

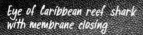
Eye of Caribbean reef shark with membrane closing

ANSWER: **True**

FISH CAN'T BLINK BECAUSE MOST DON'T HAVE EYELIDS. Some species of sharks do have eyelids, but they aren't used to blink. Instead, the **sharks partially close them when they need to protect their eyes**—usually during feeding or if they get into a fight. **Other species of fish have clear membranes over their eyes,** kind of like a window. Some shark species have this, too. The membranes slide down to protect the eye when the fish is threatened.

Instant Genius
Humans blink about every four seconds.

What are
Saturn's rings
made of?

a. metals and gas   **b.** rocks and ice   **c.** dust and gas

ANSWER: **b**

rocks and ice

SCIENTISTS KNOW THAT SATURN'S RINGS ARE MADE OF ROCKS AND ICE, but they don't know why the planet has rings or exactly how they got there. It's possible that the rock and ice pieces are left over from when Saturn formed, or they could be pieces of Saturn's moons that broke off when they were hit by asteroids. **From a distance, it looks like there are seven large rings.** But a closer review reveals that Saturn has many thinner rings around it. Scientists aren't sure of the precise number, **but it could be as many as 1,000.** The ice and rock pieces that make up Saturn's rings are different sizes. **Some are as tiny as dust, while others are huge—as big as a house!**

How tall is the tallest roller coaster in the United States?

#14

a. more than 350 feet (107 m)

b. more than 450 feet (137 m)

c. more than 550 feet (168 m)

ANSWER: b

more than 450 feet (137 m)

THE KINGDA KA ROLLER COASTER AT SIX FLAGS GREAT ADVENTURE IN NEW JERSEY IS NOT FOR ANYONE AFRAID OF HEIGHTS. At 456 feet (139 m), it is the tallest roller coaster in the United States. The towering ride is also **the second-fastest coaster on Earth,** zooming to 128 miles an hour (206 kmh) in under four seconds. Once it gets to the top of its tracks, the coaster plunges straight down.

NOW YOU KNOW!

Reaching speeds of 149 miles an hour (240 kmh), Formula Rossa at Ferrari World in the United Arab Emirates is another of the fastest roller coasters in the world.

How many **facial** **expressions** can a dog make?

a. 45

b. 100

c. 120

Pretty please?

IN ADDITION TO COMMUNICATING THROUGH TAIL WAGGING AND PLAY-BOWING, dogs use their faces and ears to communicate through more than 100 different expressions. **A pup that's feeling friendly will have its ears up and relaxed.** If its ears are relaxed and slightly forward, it could mean the dog is checking out something. **Ears that are pricked far forward can mean two things:** "Let's play" or—if the body is stiff and the dog is showing teeth—"Back off." **A dog's eyes can also "say" a lot.** Gentle eye contact is a sign of friendliness, whereas a stare may mean aggression.

NOW YOU KNOW!
When your pup rolls over to expose its belly, it's saying "I surrender," or, just as likely, "Belly rub, please!"

#16

True or False:

There is a
hotel made
entirely of

ice.

THE ORIGINAL ICE HOTEL WAS BUILT IN THE NORTHERN TOWN OF JUKKASJÄRVI, SWEDEN, IN 1989. It is rebuilt each winter, when some **1,300 blocks of ice** are taken from the nearby Torne River for the hotel's construction. The main building is made of a combination of snow and ice. Approximately 1.2 million cubic feet (30,000 m³) of material, **the equivalent to 700 million snowballs,** is used to build the floor, walls, and roofs of the hotel. The **crystal chandeliers sparkle with 1,000 hand-sculped ice crystals.** There's even a restaurant that serves food on plates of ice!

Instant Genius

Other countries, including Japan, Canada, Norway, and Finland, have ice hotels, too.

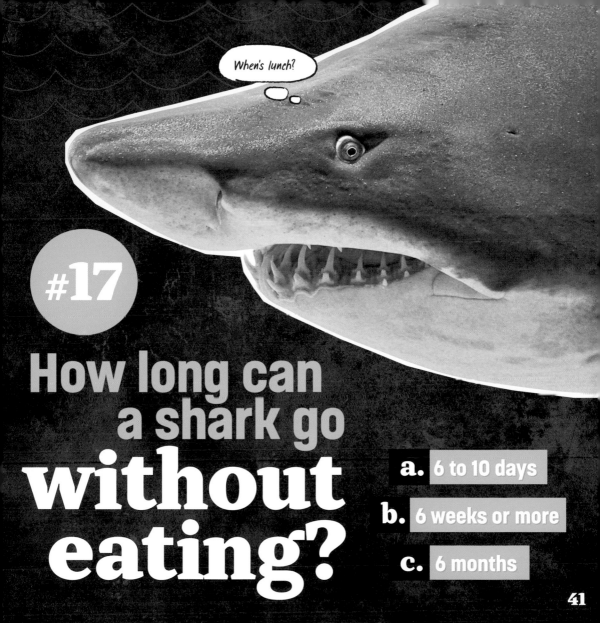

Whale shark

ANSWER: b   **6 weeks or more**

MOST SHARKS EAT EVERY TWO OR THREE DAYS, ALTHOUGH SOME CAN GO UP TO SIX WEEKS OR MORE WITHOUT A PROPER MEAL. Without food, **a shark can survive on the oil produced by its liver,** which is filled with nutrients. A shark's teeth will tell you a lot about its eating habits. **Different sharks have different kinds of teeth tailored to their preferred prey.** Great white sharks, for example, have rows of razor-sharp, triangular teeth that are serrated, like a bread knife. They are ideal for slashing through fatty fish such as tuna and mammals such as seals. **Whale sharks, on the other hand, have tiny teeth.** To feed, they don't tear into food. Instead, they use gills that filter water to sift out microscopic plankton to eat.

NOW YOU KNOW!

The megalodon was one of the largest sharks that ever lived. Its name means "giant tooth," which is very fitting considering its teeth were up to 7 inches (18 cm) long.

Up to 7 inches

Instant Genius

Scientists discovered a swell shark that hadn't eaten for 15 months but still survived.

What is Marie Curie known for?

a. She was a scientist whose research helped save many lives.

b. She was the first woman to break an Olympic record.

c. She was the first female fighter pilot in World War II.

She was a scientist whose research helped save many lives.

MARIE CURIE WAS BORN IN WARSAW, POLAND, IN 1867. She studied physics at the University of Paris at a time when almost no women were pursuing careers in science. **During her research, she discovered two chemical elements, polonium, and radium.** Radium releases radiation, a type of energy that has many uses, such as making x-rays. During World War I, Curie helped equip ambulances with x-ray machines and often **drove to field hospitals on the battlefront to make sure soldiers could get x-rays.** Radiation in controlled doses can save lives, but too much can be poisonous, though people didn't know this at the time. In the course of her work, **Curie was exposed to very high amounts of it.** She died at the age of 66 because of her exposure.

Instant Genius

Marie Curie was the first woman to win the Nobel Prize. She went on to win a second Nobel Prize, too.

lung x-ray

Mosquitos prefer biting people who have smelly feet.

#19

And you wonder why I'm a sports fan!

ANSWER: **True**

STINKY FEET MIGHT TURN YOUR FRIENDS AWAY, BUT MOSQUITOES WILL BE MORE THAN HAPPY TO KEEP YOU COMPANY. When looking for a tasty meal, mosquitoes rely not on sight but on their sense of smell to detect food. And experts have found that **specific bacteria that grow on human feet attract them!** Scientists are interested in studying mosquito behavior because malaria, a mosquito-borne illness, kills around 400,000 people worldwide every year. **Researchers are creating traps with artificially created foot odor,** hoping to lure these insects away from people and help save lives.

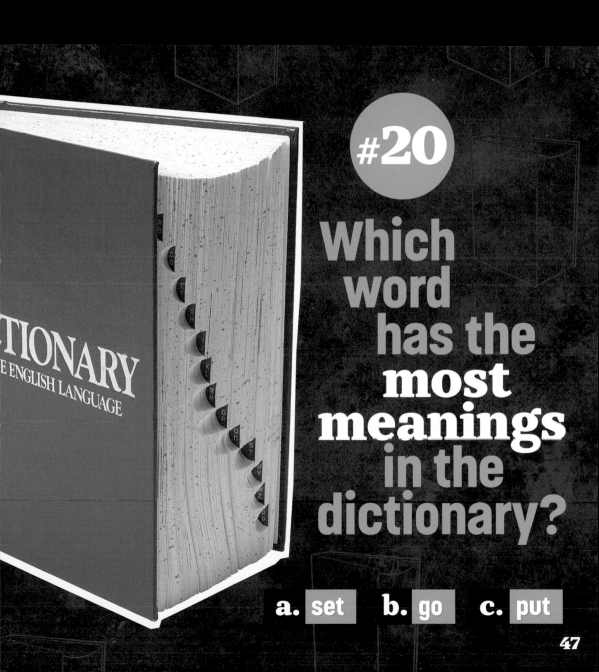

ANSWER: a

set

ACCORDING TO THE *OXFORD ENGLISH DICTIONARY*, the words "set," "run," and "put" have more meanings than any other words in the English language. **The word "set" comes out on top, with 430 definitions.** However, in the dictionary's third edition, which is slated **to be published in 2037, the word "run" will be the new record holder** for having the most definitions: a total of 645 meanings. "Go" has 368 definitions and "put" has 268. **Other words with many meanings include "get," "take," "turn," "fall," "strike," and "stand."**

Instant Genius

The dictionary adds new words each year. In 2020, it added "Covid-19," social distancing," and "elbow bump."

#21

Who has
more
**taste
buds:**
girls or boys?

a. **Boys do.**

b. **Girls do.**

c. **They have the same number.**

49

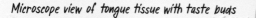
Microscope view of tongue tissue with taste buds

NOW YOU KNOW!
Humans can detect five basic tastes: sweet, salty, sour, bitter, and umami—a savory flavor.

ANSWER: **b**

Girls do.

TASTE BUDS ARE THE SENSORY ORGANS FOUND ON YOUR TONGUE, ON THE WALLS OF YOUR MOUTH, AND IN YOUR THROAT. In a taste test done in Denmark, boys and girls were given different foods to figure out who had more sensitive taste buds. They found **boys needed food to be 10 to 20 percent more sour or sweet** to detect the amount of flavor girls could. Taste buds die off and regrow about every two weeks, and as you age you have fewer of them.

Instant Genius
Eighty percent of what we taste is actually a result of our sense of smell.

#22

How old is the oldest-known living tree?

a. nearly 500 years old

b. nearly 1,500 years old

c. nearly 5,000 years old

ANSWER: C

nearly 5,000 years old

NEARLY 5,000 YEARS AGO ON A CALIFORNIA MOUNTAINSIDE, A TINY SEEDLING WAS BURROWING INTO THE SOIL AND TAKING ROOT. Today that seedling is a **Great Basin bristlecone pine tree known as Methuselah (muh-THOO-suh-luh)**—named for the longest-lived person in the Bible. This tree is so special that **the United States Forest Service keeps its exact location a secret.** Botanists (scientists who study plants) think one of the reasons the tree has lived so long is that it conserves energy by growing very, very slowly.

Instant Genius

When Methuselah was a tiny seedling, the Egyptian pyramids were being built.

**NOW
YOU KNOW!**
Female seahorses don't
give birth, males do.
Male seahorses have a
pouch on their stomachs
used to carry babies.

ANSWER: b

They growl.

**WITH THEIR LONG FACES AND
CURLY TAILS, SEAHORSES
ARE UNIQUE-LOOKING LITTLE
CREATURES.** Seahorses don't have
teeth or even a stomach. They feed
constantly by sucking as many as
3,000 tiny brine shrimp and other
small crustaceans daily through their
trumpetlike snouts. **These snouts
also emit a tiny, deep growl-like
sound when a seahorse is captured.**
The sound is too quiet to signal a
warning to other seahorses. Instead,
scientists think that the growl is
simply a way they release stress.

**Instant
Genius**
Baby seahorses are
called "fry."

How does the Moroccan

flic-flac spider

#24

escape danger?

I'm outta here!

a. It swings on its web.

b. It jumps on the back of a camel.

c. It does a summersault.

ANSWER: **c**

It does a summersault.

IF THE ANIMAL WORLD HELD AN OLYMPICS, *CEBRENNUS RECHENBERGI*, COMMONLY KNOWN AS THE MOROCCAN FLIC-FLAC SPIDER, would certainly win a medal for gymnastics. **A species of huntsman spider,** flic-flacs live in the sand dunes of the Moroccan desert, in northwestern Africa. **They hide from predators and the sun during the day by burrowing in the sand** and come out at night to hunt for moths. If threatened, a flic-flac performs some fancy acrobatics to escape. **After a running start, the spider flips through the air and lands on its hind legs.** This summersault move increases the spider's speed, helpful if it's fleeing from a predator.

Instant Genius

A robot spider inspired by the flic-flac can fold up and roll, similar to the real creature!

56

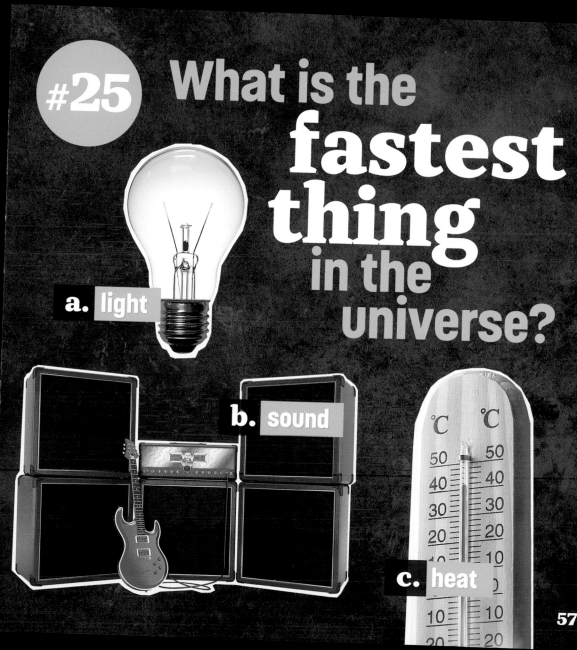

#25 What is the **fastest thing** in the **universe?**

a. light

b. sound

c. heat

57

THE SPEED OF LIGHT IS THE FASTEST THING IN THE UNIVERSE.
Light travels at a rate of about **186,000 miles a second (300,000 kms)**
when it's going through a vacuum—an area where there is nothing
to stop it, not even air. **Light travels a bit slower through air or water**
because the atoms and molecules in the air and water present an
obstacle course for light to get through. Even with something in the
way, though, light is still superfast: **It would take just one second to
go around Earth about eight times if you traveled at the speed of light.**

What does the #26
regal
horned lizard
do to protect itself?

a. It runs away.

b. It flies away.

c. It shoots blood out of its eyes.

It shoots blood out of its eyes.

SMALL AND SPIKY, REGAL HORNED LIZARDS LIVE IN THE DESERTS OF NEW MEXICO AND ARIZONA, U.S.A., AND MEXICO. They are slow runners, so it's not likely they can outpace a predator. But regal horned lizards have **other ways of defending themselves. One is camouflage,** and another is the unique ability to squirt blood from their eyes. If threatened, **this lizard can burst the blood vessels near its eyes** to trigger the surprise spray, **which can squirt about 3 feet (1 m) away.** Its target is the mouth of its predator. The blood tastes terrible, which can stop a predator from attacking.

A horned lizard camouflages itself as it lays still on the ground.

True or False:

Some Japanese bus stops are shaped like fruit.

ANSWER: True

IF YOU'RE IN JAPAN AND WAITING FOR A BUS, THERE'S A CHANCE YOU MIGHT HAVE TO DO IT IN A GIANT STRAWBERRY. In the small Japanese town of Konagai, some **bus shelters come in five different shapes—all fruits.** The bus shelters were created in the cartoonish shapes of a **watermelon, strawberry, orange, melon, and tomato** to attract visitors to a Japanese travel conference. Originally built in 1990, these quirky shelters have continued to be very popular attractions!

#28

What is the definition of a zeptosecond?

a. one zillion seconds

b. one trillionth of one billionth of a second

c. an infinite number of seconds

one trillionth of one billionth of a second

PHYSICISTS ARE SCIENTISTS WHO STUDY THE FORCES THAT MAKE EARTH AND THE UNIVERSE WORK—INCLUDING TIME. And in the world of physics, one second is a long time. When it comes to measuring time, physicists have learned how to measure even the tiniest amount. **A centisecond is a hundredth of a second, a millisecond is a thousandth of a second, and a nanosecond is a billionth of a second.** But physicists have now measured an even more microscopic bit of time: a zeptosecond, which is a trillionth of a billionth of a second.

#29

Babies yawn
before they are born.

65

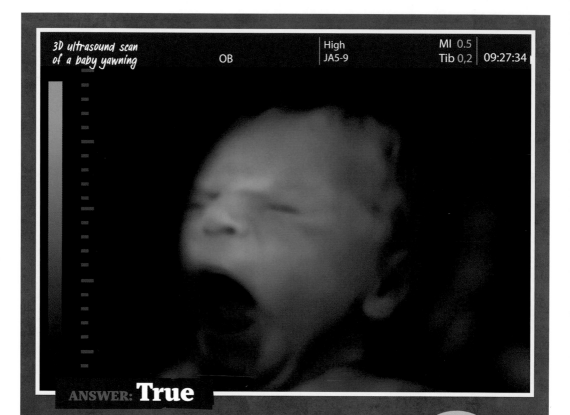

3D ultrasound scan
of a baby yawning

OB

High
JA5-9

MI 0.5
Tib 0,2 | 09:27:34

ANSWER: **True**

RESEARCHERS HAVE CONFIRMED THAT BABIES CAN YAWN WHILE DEVELOPING IN THE WOMB. When we yawn, we stretch our mouths open slowly, then close them quickly. We do it when we are sleepy, bored, and even hungry. But experts are still trying to figure out *why* we yawn. **Scientists think babies yawn for an important reason: It helps their brains develop.** But they are still trying to learn more. **In the womb, babies also suck their thumbs and hiccup.**

Instant Genius
Babies in the womb first open their eyes at around 26 weeks.

How long would it take to **drive** from Earth **to the moon?**

#30

a. **6 months**

b. **6 years**

c. **60 years**

6 months

ON AVERAGE THE MOON IS ABOUT 238,855 MILES (384,400 KM) AWAY. Driving at 60 miles an hour (97 kmh), the journey would take about six months—about the same amount of time it would take to drive around the circumference of Earth 10 times. **The only actual way to get to the moon, of course, is by spacecraft,** which would take about three days. That's what NASA astronauts did in 1969. After numerous spaceflights to prepare for a moon landing, the United States' Apollo 11 was the first crewed mission to land on the moon.

NOW YOU KNOW!

Driving straight up at 60 miles an hour (97 kmh), it would take only about an hour to leave Earth's atmosphere and reach space.

What happens if an earthworm is split in two?

#31

a. It dies.

b. It becomes two worms.

c. One half dies, while the other half might live.

ANSWER: **C**

One half dies, while the other half might live.

BOTH ENDS OF AN EARTHWORM MAY APPEAR THE SAME, BUT DON'T BE FOOLED, earthworms have a head at one end and a tail at the other. If you look closely, **the earthworm has a swollen band, which is closer to the end where the head is.** If the worm is cut behind the band, the head of the worm may survive and regrow its tail. The other half of the worm, with the original tail, will die.

Instant Genius
Researchers have found that earthworms can feel pain.

NOW YOU KNOW!
Earthworms keep soil healthy by pooping! When they poop, minerals and other nutrients are moved around underground.

#32

How long does it take a **pineapple** to grow?

a. two weeks

b. two years

c. more than a year

more than a year

PINEAPPLES GROW ON THE GROUND IN WARM, TROPICAL CLIMATES. It takes more than a year—around 13 to 18 months—for a pineapple plant to produce its fruit. **Each plant produces only a single pineapple at a time.** When pineapples are ripe, farmers pick them one at a time by hand. **They must wear protective gloves** because the long leaves of the plant are very sharp.

NOW YOU KNOW!
Unlike other fruits, pineapples don't ripen any more after picking. When you take one home from the grocery store, it's as ready to eat as it'll ever be.

#33

What percentage of British people

drink tea every day?

a. about 75 percent

b. about 60 percent

c. about 45 percent

about 75 percent

Portugal's Princess Catherine introduced tea to Britain.

TEA IS ONE OF THE MOST POPULAR DRINKS IN BRITAIN. In fact, about 75 percent of British people drink tea every day. **Tea became popular in Britain after the daughter of Portugal's king married Britain's king in 1662.** The new queen brought several crates of loose-leaf tea with her from Portugal, as the Portuguese had been importing tea from China since the 16th century, and tea was popular with the royal society. The British had already been introduced to tea but only as medicine that was thought to make the body feel strong. **It didn't become popular until the new queen began drinking it daily,** including at social gatherings. Seeing the queen drink tea made other women want to drink it, too.

Instant Genius

China produces more tea than any other country in the world.

#34

True or False:

Octopuses
and squid
have
beaks.

An octopus's suckers can taste what they touch.

Beak

ANSWER: **True**

NOW YOU KNOW!
Giant squids have the largest eyes of any other animal on Earth. Each eye is about the size of a 10-inch (25-cm) dinner plate.

OCTOPUSES AND SQUID HAVE A MOUTH LOCATED IN THE CENTER OF THEIR RING OF EIGHT ARMS. And directly inside their mouths, they have **hard beaks similar to a parrot's.** After they capture a meal with their muscular arms, they use their beaks and spiky tongues to break through the tough shell of their prey. **The beaks are the only hard parts in these animals' bodies,** which explains why octopuses and squid are excellent escape artists: Any small space an octopus or squid can fit its beak into, it can fit its entire body through.

How long is the Great Wall of China?

a. more than 13 miles (21 km)

b. more than 33 miles (53 km)

c. more than 13,000 miles (21,000 km)

ANSWER: C

more than 13,000 miles (21,000 km)

THE GREAT WALL OF CHINA WAS BUILT TO PROTECT THE COUNTRY FROM OUTSIDE INVADERS. Chinese officials estimate that it stretches more than 13,000 miles (21,000 km), making it **the longest man-made structure in the world.** But it's hard to know for sure how long the wall actually is. Why? Parts of the wall were built on top of or next to other sections during different time periods. **The height of the wall also varies, from 15 to 30 feet (4.5 to 9 m)** high depending on the section.

NOW YOU KNOW!
Guard towers along the Great Wall were once used to send messages by using signals such as smoke or fire.

How much of the world's **oxygen** is produced in the **ocean?**

#36

a. none

b. at least 25 percent

c. at least 50 percent

at least 50 percent

Phytoplankton seen through a microscope.

SCIENTISTS ESTIMATE THAT THE OCEAN PRODUCES 50 TO 80 PERCENT OF THE WORLD'S OXYGEN. How does the ocean make so much? The answer is **microscopic plants, algae, and bacteria called plankton.** Plankton are divided into two groups: phytoplankton (made up of plants) and zooplankton (made up of animals). Like land plants, **phytoplankton use sunlight to make energy and produce oxygen in the process.** It's estimated that one particular species of plankton, called ***Prochlorococcus*, produces up to 20 percent of the world's oxygen.** That's more oxygen than is produced by all the tropical rain forests on land.

Prochlorococcus

37

How did **Rosa Parks** impact the civil rights movement?

a. She led protests all over the United States.

b. She refused to give up her seat on a bus.

c. She became the first African American woman to go to college.

She refused to give up her seat on a bus.

THE CIVIL RIGHTS MOVEMENT IN THE UNITED STATES WAS A STRUGGLE FOR EQUALITY THAT TOOK PLACE DURING THE 1950S AND 1960S. Rosa Parks was an activist during the civil rights movement who, along with her husband, worked on social justice issues. In 1955, Parks refused to give up her seat when a white person wanted to sit down on a bus. **Back then, African American people were not allowed to use the same doors, bathrooms, or bus seats as white people.** This was called segregation. Rosa Parks didn't believe this was fair, so she stayed seated in protest knowing that it would cause her to be arrested and jailed. **Her brave actions inspired many others,** Black and white, to protest, too. **In the 1960s, segregation became illegal, but there still remain issues with racism even today.** Many people continue to protest and fight for equal rights for people of all races and backgrounds.

Rosa Parks stands with civil rights leader, Dr. Martin Luther King, Jr., during a dinner honoring her.

Statue of Rosa Parks in the National Civil Rights Museum in Memphis, Tennessee

ANSWER: True

A QUEEN BEE HAS A UNIQUE LANGUAGE THAT SHE USES TO COMMUNICATE WITH HER WORKER BEES. Listening to these bees with high-tech tools, scientists discovered that **queens make noises that sound like "quack" and "toot."** A queen honeybee grows from a larva selected by worker bees. **She matures in a special wax cell** while the worker bees feed her a protein-rich jelly. When the queen is ready to hatch, **she quacks at the workers to release her. Once she's freed, she starts making a tooting sound.** This signals the workers to leave the other queens still in their wax cells as they are. The first queen out doesn't want any other queens as rivals!

Queen bee

Worker bees

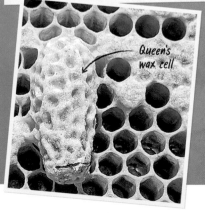

Queen's wax cell

Instant Genius

Two queens released at the same time will fight to the death.

How much **bacteria** lives on a square inch (6.5 sq cm) of your skin?

a. hundreds of bacteria

b. thousands of bacteria

c. millions of bacteria

Ultraviolet light showing bacteria and viruses on a hand that has not been washed

ANSWER: **C**

millions of bacteria

YOUR SKIN IS YOUR BODY'S LARGEST ORGAN, AND ITS JOB IS TO PROTECT YOU. The skin acts as a barrier to harmful stuff such as germs. What you might not realize is that **your skin is also an entire ecosystem full of bacteria, fungi, viruses, and even mites (teeny tiny bugs)** that together make up what is known as your skin microbiome. Your skin also helps you stay healthy in different ways, including by helping to keep your body temperature stable and producing vitamin D, which it makes from sunlight.

Staphylococcus epidermidis bacteria

How many hours a day do lions rest?

#40

a. 15 to 20

b. 10 to 12

c. 8 to 10

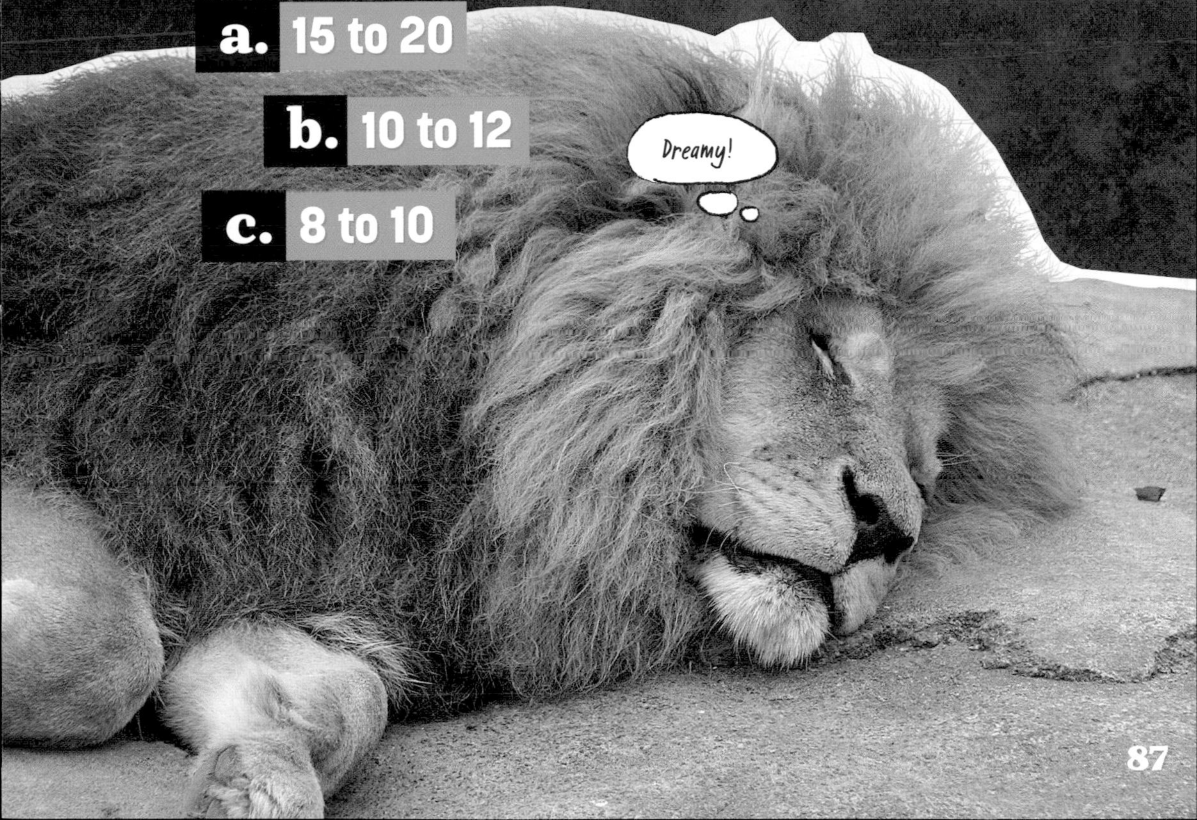

A lion's roar can be heard up to 5 miles (8 km) away.

Quit snoring.

ANSWER: a

15 to 20

AFRICAN LIONS SPEND MOST OF THEIR TIME SLEEPING ON THE SAVANNA WHERE THEY LIVE. They need to rest a lot so they are prepared to chase prey such as antelopes, wildebeests, and zebras. Why? **A lion's top speed is about 50 miles an hour (80 kmh)—but only for short bursts.** Many of the animals they go after can run as fast or faster than that, **so lions need their energy.** Lions are social animals that live in groups called prides. They usually hunt at dawn and dusk, and **females are usually the hunters.**

NOW YOU KNOW!
Lions are the second-largest cats in the world, after tigers. Like lions, tigers sleep a lot!

The *Harry Potter* books have been translated into how many languages?

41

HARRIUS POTTER

et Philosophi Lapis

J.K.ROWLING

9¾

HAMAXOSTICHUS RAPIDUS HOGVARTENSIS

a. **80**

b. **60**

c. **55**

Translation by Peter Needham

BLOOMSBURY

ANSWER: a

80

MORE THAN 500 MILLION BOOKS IN THE *HARRY POTTER* SERIES HAVE BEEN SOLD AROUND THE WORLD. They have also been translated into 80 languages, **including ancient Greek!** These stories have come to life in the movies, too. There are eight films based on the books. Before the first book in the series was published, **author J.K. Rowling pitched her idea many times.** In fact, the story was rejected 12 times before a publisher was willing to give it a chance.

J.K. Rowling

What is a

camel's
hump

filled with?

a. water   b. fat   c. bones

Dromedary camel

What do you call a camel with no humps?

NOW YOU KNOW!
Camels can drink up to 20 gallons (76 L) of water at one time. Camels also get water by absorbing it from the plants they eat.

ANSWER: **b** | **fat**

Humphrey.

Bactrian camel

THERE ARE TWO TYPES OF CAMELS:
Dromedary camels are one-humped and live in North Africa. **Bactrian camels** have two humps and live in Central Asia. Both store fat in their humps. **When food and water are scarce, a camel's body uses the fat in its hump (or humps) for energy.** If the fat is used up entirely, the hump will droop. Once the camel eats again, its hump goes back to normal. This is just one way a camel is perfectly adapted to survive in its desert home. **Camels can also completely close their nostrils during sandstorms.** To protect their eyes, they have two rows of eyelashes and three sets of eyelids. Wide feet allow them to walk across the sand without sinking into it.

Instant Genius
Camels can live for seven months without drinking water.

#43 How much did the world's first computer weigh?

a. about as much as one cocker spaniel

b. about as much as one zebra

c. about as much as 10 hippos

ANSWER: C

about as much as 10 hippos

THE NAME OF THE WORLD'S VERY FIRST COMPUTER WAS THE ELECTRONIC NUMERICAL INTEGRATOR AND COMPUTER, OR ENIAC FOR SHORT. By today's standards, it was gigantic, weighing about the same as 10 male hippos! ENIAC, which **filled a basement nearly as big as a ballroom,** started as a top-secret military project during World War II. After years of trial and error, **ENIAC was able to make a calculation in 30 seconds that took a human 20 hours to figure out.** From mobile phones and laptops to alarm clocks and cars, many things we depend on today were made faster, simpler, and more effective because there are computers inside of them that were developed using technology from ENIAC.

Instant Genius

Today, all of ENIAC's technology can fit in a microchip the size of a dime.

How much **air** do you breathe in a day?

a. enough to fill a swimming pool

b. enough to fill a bathtub

c. enough to fill a minivan

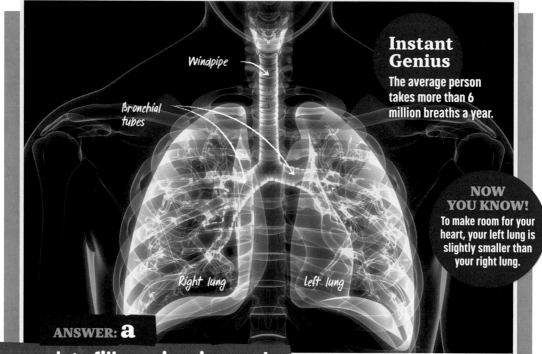

Windpipe

Bronchial
tubes

Right lung

Left lung

ANSWER: a

enough to fill a swimming pool

THE LUNGS NEVER STOP WORKING. They take in about 17,000 breaths a day, enough oxygen to fill up a swimming pool. The lungs are also one of the largest organs in the body. **When you breathe in, air moves down your windpipe into two tunnels called bronchial tubes.** The tubes split off into tinier tubes called bronchioles, which contain **small air sacs called alveoli.** The alveoli switch out the carbon dioxide for oxygen in the blood. Your diaphragm, which is a muscle in your chest, expands and contracts to move air in and out of your lungs.

Alveoli

What did the colors of the Olympic flag once represent?

#45

a. the colors of the rainbow

b. five continents

c. the colors of the medals

The Olympic flag raising ceremony at the 2018 Winter Olympics Opening Ceremony in Pyeongchang, South Korea

ANSWER: b

five continents

THE OLYMPIC FLAG WAS FIRST FLOWN AT THE 1920 SUMMER OLYMPICS IN BELGIUM. The design of red, blue, yellow, black, and green interlocking circles was initially created to represent the continents: **North and South America were combined and represented by the color red, with blue for Europe, yellow for Asia, black for Africa, and green for Australia, New Zealand, and the islands of the South Pacific Ocean, known together as Oceania.** The rings no longer represent specific continents. Today, the rings are a symbol of the coming together of countries and athletes from around the world.

Instant Genius

At least one of the five Olympic colors appears in the flag of every country in the world.

What is the

largest snake

in the world?

a. the python

b. the green anaconda

c. the black mamba

the green anaconda

WEIGHING IN AT A WHOPPING 550 POUNDS (250 KG) AND GROWING UP TO 30 FEET (9 M) LONG, green anacondas are the largest and heaviest snakes in the world. **These reptiles have survived on Earth for almost 3 million years.** They live in the swamps and streams of South America's tropical rainforests. **These snakes are strong and fast swimmers,** spending their time submerged in water with only their eyes and nasal openings showing. As soon as some unsuspecting animal strolls by for a sip of water, the snake attacks.

NOW YOU KNOW!
The green anaconda coils around its prey either to suffocate it or drag it into the water to drown it.

Instant Genius

Baby green anacondas can hunt and swim from the time they are born.

What living structure can be seen from space?

a. Australia's Great Barrier Reef

b. Central America's Belize Barrier Reef

c. Fiji's Rainbow Reef

Great Barrier Reef

Coast of Australia

ANSWER: a

Australia's Great Barrier Reef

ONE OF THE SEVEN NATURAL WONDERS OF THE WORLD, THE GREAT BARRIER REEF IS SO BIG THAT IT CAN BE SEEN FROM SPACE. It stretches 133,000 square miles (344,400 sq km), and like most reefs, **it is actually made up of a number of reefs and coral islands.** Its rich sea life includes 30 species of whales and dolphins, 6 species of sea turtles, 14 species of sea snakes, and more than 1,500 species of fish. Compared with other coral reefs, the Great Barrier Reef is on the young side: **According to scientists, it's just 500,000 years old.**

Instant Genius
The Great Barrier Reef Marine Park is home to 600 islands.

True or False:

Scorpions **glow** in the dark.

#48

103

ANSWER: True

SCORPIONS GLOW IN THE DARK BECAUSE THEY HAVE A SPECIAL LAYER OF CLEAR SKIN ON THE OUTSIDE OF THEIR BODIES that turns fluorescent in ultraviolet light, causing them to glow. Scientists have several theories as to why this happens. **The glow could be a natural sunblock.** It's also possible that **the glow confuses a scorpion's prey,** making it easier for scorpions to catch their meals. **Or perhaps the glow provides a way for scorpions to recognize one another.**

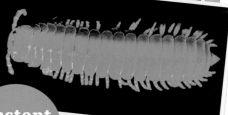

Instant Genius

Crayfish, centipedes, and millipedes are also known to glow.

Every continent except Antarctica has a city named

Rome.

ROME

Rome, Italy

ANSWER: True

THE ORIGINAL CITY OF ROME—ROMA IN ITALIAN—IS THE CAPITAL OF ITALY, IN EUROPE. There is also a Roma in Indonesia (Asia), Lesotho (Africa), Queensland (Australia), and Ecuador (South America). **In North America there are at least 13 towns named Rome,** in the U.S. states of Georgia, Illinois, Indiana, Maine, Missouri, Mississippi, New York, Iowa, Ohio, Kentucky, Oregon, Pennsylvania, and Tennessee.

What is **Harriet Tubman** known for?

a. She fought in the Revolutionary War.

b. She helped enslaved people escape to freedom.

c. She was the first African American woman to vote.

ANSWER: **b**

She helped enslaved people escape to freedom.

BORN AROUND 1820, HARRIET TUBMAN GREW UP IN A ONE-ROOM CABIN ON A MARYLAND PLANTATION WITH HER NINE BROTHERS AND SISTERS. In 1849, Harriet discovered that she along with other enslaved people on the plantation were going to be sold. She decided to run away. During this time, **enslaved people used a secret route called the Underground Railroad to flee to freedom** from the southern slave states to the northern free states. **This was not an actual train but rather a number of safe locations where people would help travelers hide as they journeyed.** Harriet successfully escaped to Pennsylvania, a free state. After that, **she repeatedly risked her life,** going back into slave states to free other enslaved people.

Statue of Harriet Tubman in New York City

#51

How
hot
does it get
on Earth's
moon?

a. 150°F (66°C)

b. 250°F (120°C)

c. 300°F (149°C)

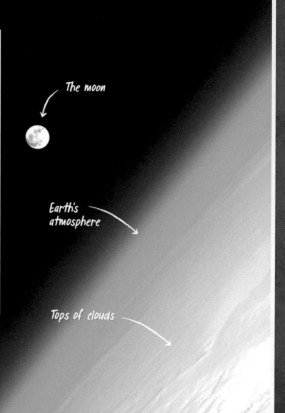

The moon and Earth's atmosphere as seen from the International Space Station

ANSWER:

ANSWER: **b**

250°F (120°C)

TEMPERATURES ON THE MOON ARE EXTREME. During the day, near the moon's equator, temperatures can reach a scorching 250°F (120°C). **At night, it can dip to a frigid –208°F (–130°C). And the moon's north and south poles get even colder.** This huge swing in temperature happens because, unlike Earth, **the moon doesn't have much of an atmosphere** (a blanket of gases protecting it from the sun's heat and the freezing temperatures of space). Earth's atmosphere not only helps control temperature; it also has the oxygen we need to breathe.

The moon

Earth's atmosphere

Tops of clouds

Instant Genius
The moon is Earth's closest neighbor in space.

110

#52

How much **spit** does your mouth create in a day?

a. as much as one cup (237 mL)

b. as much as one pint (473 mL)

c. as much as one quart (946 mL)

as much as one quart (946 mL)

ALL OVER THE INSIDE OF YOUR MOUTH ARE HUNDREDS OF LITTLE GLANDS THAT LOOK LIKE TINY WATER BALLOONS. These are salivary glands, and they keep your mouth wet by producing as much as one quart (946 mL) saliva, or spit, every day. **Saliva is 99 percent water mixed with other ingredients, such as salts.** Saliva is very useful: It contains the minerals calcium, fluoride, and phosphate that protect your teeth against cavities. **Saliva also helps your mouth heal** after you lose a tooth or if you have a small cut. Saliva even helps you talk by allowing your cheeks, lips, and tongue to move around your mouth without sticking to your teeth.

Instant Genius

In one year, a person can make enough saliva to fill two bathtubs.

Antarctica

belongs to which country?

a. It belongs to the United Kingdom.

b. It belongs to New Zealand.

c. It doesn't belong to any country.

ANSWER: C

It doesn't belong to any country.

ANTARCTICA IS THE COLDEST, WINDIEST, AND DRIEST CONTINENT ON EARTH. It does not have its own government, flag, or permanent residents. No country owns it, but the United States, Australia, Chile, China, and many others have agreed to share land there. This international agreement, called the Antarctic Treaty, says that **the world's fifth-largest continent is considered a scientific preserve.** The only people in Antarctica are scientists performing research or tourists visiting the vast, icy land. **Antarctica is home to a variety of animals, including penguins, leopard and elephant seals, orcas, and blue whales.**

Instant Genius

Antarctica contains 90 percent of Earth's ice.

#54

True or False:

Giraffes
make very
few noises.

ANSWER: **True**

ZOOKEEPERS AND WILDLIFE EXPERTS HAVE RARELY HEARD SO MUCH AS A PEEP COMING FROM A GIRAFFE—aside from the occasional snort. Giraffes do have a voice box, but because their tracheas—the tube that connects the windpipe to the lungs—are so long, **they are not able to get enough airflow to vibrate their vocal cords to make sounds.** New research, however, has found that **these gentle giants hum at night.** The hum is too low for human ears to hear, but—thanks to technology—the sounds have been recorded so scientists can study them.

Instant Genius
Giraffes have great eyesight.

#55

How fast can an **avalanche** move?

a. 200 miles an hour (320 kmh)

b. 95 miles an hour (153 kmh)

c. 65 miles an hour (105 kmh)

NOW YOU KNOW!
Avalanches are less likely to happen on slopes with lots of trees and large rocks, which help keep snow attached to the mountain.

DANGER AVALANCHE

ANSWER: **a**

200 miles an hour (320 kmh)

AN AVALANCHE IS A LARGE MASS OF SNOW THAT MOVES DOWNHILL, SWEEPING AWAY EVERYTHING IN ITS PATH. It occurs when **a thick, heavy slab of snow lying on top of a weaker layer of snow breaks off** and slides down a slope, picking up speed as it goes and reaching up to 200 miles an hour (320 kmh). Natural forces such as heavy snowfall or rainfall, rapid changes in temperature, and strong winds can cause snow to loosen. Falling rocks, ice, or trees can also trigger an avalanche, and **so can skiers, snowboarders, and skimobiles.**

Instant Genius
About 100,000 avalanches occur each year in the western United States.

How high is Olympus Mons, the largest volcano in our solar system?

a. 1.6 miles (2.6 km) high

b. 6 miles (10 km) high

c. 16 miles (25 km) high

An illustration of Olympus Mons

ANSWER: C

16 miles (25 km) high

OLYMPUS MONS IS AN EXTINCT VOLCANO LOCATED ON MARS. At 16 miles (25 km) high and 374 miles (602 km) wide, it is the largest volcano in our solar system. **Olympus Mons is so big it could entirely cover the U.S. state of Arizona!** By comparison, **the largest volcano on Earth is Mauna Loa, in Hawaii.** It's 6.3 miles (10 km) high and 75 miles (120 km) wide.

Mauna loa

NOW YOU KNOW!

Though Mauna Loa is the *largest* mountain on Earth, Mount Everest—which rises 29,032 feet (8,849 m)—is the *highest* point on our planet.

True or False:

A chameleon
changes its color to camouflage itself.

How do I look?

#57

Instant Genius
Chameleons have very sticky spit, to help them grab their prey.

ANSWER: **False**

THE IDEA THAT CHAMELEONS CHANGE COLOR TO MATCH THEIR ENVIRONMENT IS A MYTH. Instead, these reptiles transform as a response to mood, temperature, and light. Chameleons can't make their own body heat; **changing their skin color is a way to regulate their body temperature.** In cooler weather, a chameleon may become dark to absorb more heat. In warmer weather, a chameleon may turn pale to reflect the sun's rays away and keep cool. **Chameleons also use color changes to communicate with one another.** Males become bright to show they are in charge. Females change color to show they are ready to mate.

NOW YOU KNOW!
Chameleons can move each of their eyes independently, allowing them to see in every direction at once.

Who was the youngest person ever to have received the Nobel Peace Prize?

#58

a. Mother Teresa

b. Malala Yousafzai

c. Barack Obama

Malala Yousafzai

WHEN MALALA WAS 11 YEARS OLD, SHE WROTE A BLOG POST about her fear of being a girl going to school in her hometown in the country of Pakistan. Under strict rules set by an extremist group called the Taliban, **women and girls were not allowed to speak their minds.** The Taliban also wanted to stop girls from getting an education. But Malala knew this was wrong, so **she continued to write about and eventually speak out about the importance of educating all girls.** The Taliban became angry at Malala for her activism and sent men to silence her. **Despite being shot, Malala survived and kept speaking her mind.** By age 17, Malala was the youngest person ever to be awarded the prestigious Nobel Peace Prize.

Instant Genius

Today, Malala travels the world encouraging girls to attend school.

How fast does a rocket need to travel to escape Earth's gravity?

a. 25,000 miles an hour (40,000 kmh)

b. 5,000 miles an hour (8,000 kmh)

c. 500 miles an hour (800 kmh)

ANSWER: a

25,000 miles an hour (40,000 kmh)

FOR A ROCKET TO LEAVE EARTH AND ENTER ORBIT, it needs to be moving at least 25,000 miles an hour (40,000 kmh) to burst free from Earth's gravitational force. **Making this happen is one of the biggest and most expensive challenges facing space travel.** The heavier an object, the more fuel it takes to lift it. But fuel is heavy, too. This requires even more power for liftoff. **Scientists at NASA are working to break this cycle of speed, fuel, and weight** by inventing lighter space vehicles, more efficient fuel, and new and improved propulsion, or takeoff, methods.

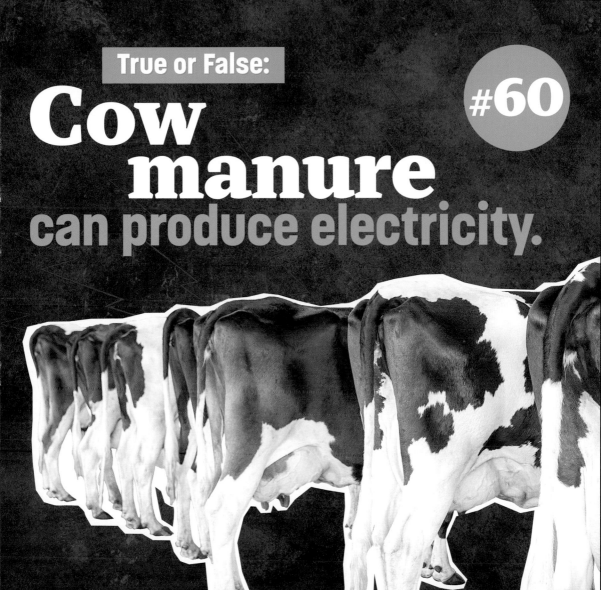

True or False:

Cow manure

can produce electricity.

127

Cow manure being collected to extract methane to produce electricity

ANSWER: True

MANURE FROM COWS CAN PRODUCE ENERGY, INCLUDING ELECTRICITY. In fact, people have experimented with converting manure into energy for hundreds of years. Over the past few decades, new technologies have made this easier and safer for the environment. **Today, cow manure can be burned to power steam engines. It is also converted into a gas called methane.** Bacteria is used to break down the manure, which produces the gas. Methane gas can then be used to make electricity. **Any leftover manure can be turned into fertilizer, used to grow crops.**

WILLKOMMEN IN HELLABRUNN

Instant Genius

The Munich Zoo in Germany uses animal manure to power the zoo.

What percentage of all species that have ever lived

no longer exist?

a. more than 9 percent

b. more than 19 percent

c. more than 99 percent

NOW YOU KNOW! Human activities such as building cities and driving cars has taken resources away from animals, contributing to the extinction of many species.

IT'S ESTIMATED THAT THERE ARE 8.7 MILLION SPECIES OF PLANTS AND ANIMALS LIVING ON EARTH. That seems like a lot. And yet scientists believe that more than 99 percent of all species that ever lived are now extinct. All of the living things that exist today developed and changed over many years from earlier types; **animals changing over time to survive where they live is called evolution.** When a living thing changes, or adapts, to survive its environment, it passes along those adaptations to its offspring. **Many animals that are not able to adapt to a changing environment eventually die off.** Others might relocate to a different place if their environment is no longer suitable. Some even change their bodies or behavior in order to adapt.

Instant Genius
Due to climate change and other factors, wolverines are under threat of extinction.

Wolverine

#62 How many liters of **fresh water** does it take to make 1 liter of **bottled soda?**

a. 1 liter

b. 1.5 liters

c. 2 liters

ANSWER: C

2 liters

THE REASON IT TAKES 2 LITERS OF WATER TO MAKE JUST 1 LITER OF SODA IS BECAUSE THE PROCESS OF MAKING THE PLASTIC SODA BOTTLE USES WATER. Every product we use has a "water footprint," which is a calculation that adds up all of the water needed to produce something. Manufacturing, assembling, and packaging all involve using water. **To make 1 pound (0.5 kg) of plastic, it takes 22 gallons (83 L) of water.** And because of all the small parts needed to build a smartphone, it takes 3,190 gallons (12,075 L) of water to make just one of them.

What was
Quetzalcoatlus?

a. the world's largest flying reptile

b. an award-winning chocolate dessert recipe

c. an ancient city

#63

the world's largest flying reptile

AS TALL AS A GIRAFFE AND WITH A WINGSPAN AS WIDE AS A SMALL AIRPLANE, *Quetzalcoatlus* was one of the largest animals ever to fly. Known as a pterosaur, this ancient airborne reptile weighed only about 200 pounds (90 kg)—not very heavy, given how huge it was. This is because it had hollow bones. **Named after the Aztec feathered serpent god, Quetzalcóatl,** *Quetzalcoatlus* lived at the same time as the dinosaurs. **It died out with the dinosaurs, too—about 66 million years ago.**

NOW YOU KNOW!
A fossilized part of *Quetzalcoatlus*'s wing was discovered by a geology graduate student in a national park in Texas, U.S.A.

Statue of Quetzalcoatl

An illustration of Quetzalcoatlus

True or False:

Space has a smell.

#64

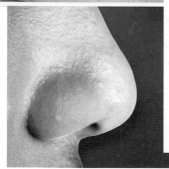

ANSWER: True

GETTING A GOOD LONG WHIFF OF SPACE AIR IS IMPOSSIBLE.
Without a space suit, an astronaut would last only about 15 seconds before passing out from lack of oxygen. However, **astronauts have noted the scent of seared steak, walnuts, and burning metal** that linger in a space shuttle's airlocks when they return from space walks and remove their helmets. These smells are important because they can give us hints about what our galaxy is made of. One theory is that **the unusual scents could come from dying stars that produce smelly compounds that float around the universe.**

True or False:

It's illegal to have a

pet rat

in Alberta, Canada.

#65

IF YOU ARE CONSIDERING RAISING A PET RAT, DO NOT MOVE TO ALBERTA. In 1950, the province in western Canada declared rats to be pests—animals that are likely to destroy crops or livestock. The province's Agricultural Pests Act made it **mandatory for property owners to report or destroy any rat they encountered.** And Canadians were up to the challenge: Rat patrols cruised Alberta's border with the province of Saskatchewan, to the east, leaving poison for these rodents. **Today, there is a phone number and an email address for Canadians in Alberta to report rat sightings.** If a rat appears, the event is in the news for days.

you Can't Ignore the RAT

He's a menace to **HEALTH** HE CARRIES GERMS **HOME** HE DESTROYS PROPERTY **INDUSTRY** HE CAUSES WASTE

KILL HIM!

LET'S KEEP ALBERTA RAT-FREE

THE DIVISION OF ENTOMOLOGY, DEPARTMENT OF PUBLIC HEALTH, EDMONTON

Instant Genius

Anyone caught with a pet rat in Alberta is fined thousands of dollars.

True or False:

Humans and other mammals **cry** when upset.

#66

ANSWER: False

MANY ANIMALS HAVE THE ABILITY TO MAKE TEARS. They do so to keep their eyes moist. **And all mammals make crying-like calls,** such as when a baby wants its mother. But when it comes to emotional crying, **humans are the only species who cry to express sadness.** But that doesn't mean animals can't express sadness in other ways. Great apes, for example, show grief when another dies by carrying the body around. **Researchers have also seen elephants grieving in the wild.** Mother elephants will refuse to leave behind a weak or dying calf. They will show grief through their eyes, which will look sunken, and in their ears, which will droop.

What is **belly button lint** partly made out of?

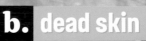

a. animal fur

b. dead skin

c. dust bunnies

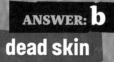

ANSWER: b
dead skin

BELLY BUTTON LINT IS MADE UP OF DEAD SKIN CELLS, BODY HAIR, AND STRAY CLOTHING FIBERS. The belly button **forms after birth when the umbilical cord is cut and the skin heals as scar tissue.** In about 90 percent of people, the skin heals to form a belly button that caves in, an "innie." In roughly the other 10 percent, the scar tissue heals differently, resulting in a belly button that might stick out a bit, known as an "outie." **Women tend to get less lint than men** because they have less body hair, which is what causes the lint to stick.

Instant Genius
All mammals have belly buttons.

#68

True or False:

Dolphins **shut down** half their brains when they sleep.

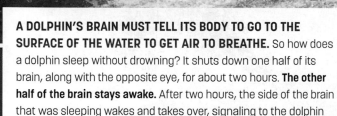

ANSWER: True

A DOLPHIN'S BRAIN MUST TELL ITS BODY TO GO TO THE SURFACE OF THE WATER TO GET AIR TO BREATHE. So how does a dolphin sleep without drowning? It shuts down one half of its brain, along with the opposite eye, for about two hours. **The other half of the brain stays awake.** After two hours, the side of the brain that was sleeping wakes and takes over, signaling to the dolphin that **it's time to rise to the surface for air.**

Instant Genius
Sometimes dolphins sleep on the water's surface where it's easier to get air.

144

True or False:

#69

If a frog eats a firefly, it can

glow.

145

THE NEXT TIME YOU SEE A FROG THAT LOOKS LIKE IT HAS A NIGHT LIGHT GLOWING IN ITS BELLY, chances are it has eaten a firefly. **Frogs swallow their food whole, which means after a frog swallows a firefly, the insect can still emit a glow.** Sometimes we can see that glow because frogs have thin skin. **There are more than 2,000 species of fireflies, but only some of them make light.** Their light can be yellow, orange, green, or even blue. Males glow to introduce themselves to females, and females glow back to help the males find them.

Instant Genius

Despite their names, fireflies aren't flies at all. They're beetles.

True or False:

Cosmic dust

from space falls to Earth.

70

WHENEVER YOU GO OUTSIDE, INVISIBLE DUST IS FALLING FROM THE SKY. Some of this dust comes from space. **It's leftover pieces of rock from the formation of the planets in our solar system and debris from comets and asteroids.** Scientists are still trying to figure out exactly how much space dust falls to Earth. Some estimate it could be about 120,000 pounds (54,400 kg) a day. Others estimate closer to 220,000 pounds (99,800 kg) a day. **If falling particles are more than 2 millimeters in diameter, they are visible as what we call a shooting star.** But most space dust is teeny tiny and can't be seen with the naked eye.

Instant Genius

Though most stardust falls to the ground, it's possible that we breathe in tiny amounts of it.

#71

True or False:

A city's major league sports teams always share the

same team colors.

ANSWER: **False**

PITTSBURGH, PENNSYLVANIA, IS THE ONLY CITY
IN THE UNITED STATES WHOSE MAJOR LEAGUE
SPORTS TEAMS SHARE THE SAME TEAM COLORS.
There, the Pirates (baseball), the Steelers (football),
and the Penguins (hockey) **all have gold and black on
their uniforms, which are the colors in Pittsburgh's flag.**
Sports are a huge deal in Pittsburgh. In fact, the Pirates
played against the Boston Americans in the very first
World Series baseball game, which took place in 1903.

Instant Genius

Pittsburgh is known as the City
of Bridges: It has 446 of them!

#72

Animals are

ticklish.

ANSWER: **True**

THERE ARE TWO KINDS OF TICKLING. The light touch that feels like a feather and makes you feel itchy is called knismesis. Many animals react in a way that shows they feel this kind of tickle. If you lightly touch your dog's paw, for example, it may yank it away quickly. **Horses shudder to shake flies off their backs.** The second kind of tickling, which makes us laugh, is called gargalesis. Chimps and gorillas have been observed experiencing this kind of tickling. **Scientists believe that gargalesis evolved as social bonding between parents and their young.** They also believe that tickle fights help youngsters develop self-defense skills.

#73

How much of the human brain is made of **water?**

a. 20 percent b. 30 percent c. 75 percent

ANSWER: C

75 percent

THE HUMAN BRAIN IS ABOUT 75 PERCENT WATER. Your brain manages your body's functions, including processing information, feeling emotions, and making decisions. **To work properly, the brain needs a constant supply of oxygen, which it gets from the water in blood.** The more energy your brain uses, the more oxygen your brain will use from your blood. **In adults, about a quarter of a gallon (1 L) of blood flows through the brain every minute.** This is enough to fill half of a 2-liter bottle of soda.

Instant Genius
The human body overall is 60 percent water.

True or False:

largest rock

The in the world is 1,142 feet (348 m) tall.

#74

True

Uluru seen from the
International Space Station

**ULURU, THE LARGEST SINGLE STANDING
ROCK ON EARTH, IS ACTUALLY
1,142 FEET (348 M) TALL.** It's even higher
than the Eiffel Tower in Paris, France! **Uluru
is located in the desert of central Australia.**
It contains caves at it base where ancient
paintings and carvings created by
Indigenous Australians have been found.
**This artwork and the rock itself are sacred
to these people who have lived in the area
more than 30,000 years.**

**Instant
Genius**

Uluru is 300 million years old.

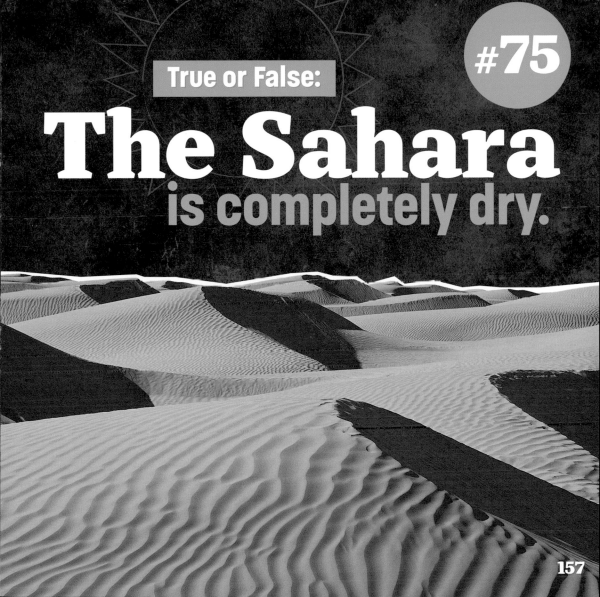

True or False:

The Sahara
is completely dry.

#75

WHEN MOST PEOPLE THINK OF THE SAHARA, THEY PROBABLY PICTURE GIGANTIC SAND DUNES. But those dunes cover only about 20 percent of the desert. The Sahara might be one of the driest environments on Earth, but water *does* exist there. **Two large rivers—the Nile and the Niger—run through the Sahara,** which blankets one third of the African continent. **There are also many lakes and aquifers (natural sources of underground water)** that fill up and then dry out depending on the season.

Lake at Umm al-Maa, Libyan Sahara

Atlantic Ocean

Mediterranean Sea

Sahara

Nile River

Niger River

Red Sea

NOW YOU KNOW!

The Sahara is bordered on three sides by water: the Mediterranean Sea to the north, the Atlantic Ocean to the west, and the Red Sea to the east.

True or False:

Carrots
have always been orange.

#76

NOW
YOU KNOW!

Orange carrots get their
color from beta-carotene,
a nutrient that is full of an
orange-red pigment. Sweet
potatoes and pumpkins
have beta-carotene,
too.

ANSWER: **False**

CARROTS WERE NOT ALWAYS ORANGE. Wild carrots, which
grew in parts of Europe, western Asia, and northern Africa,
were once purple or yellow. People in western Asia began
cultivating them about 5,000 years ago—the first evidence
we have of carrots being grown for food. The new carrots
were brought from Asia to what is now Spain and, eventually,
to other parts of Europe. **The Dutch began growing orange
carrots in the 1600s,** and they are now the most popular color,
though purple and yellow carrots are still available.

**Instant
Genius**
Scientists believe the
nutrients in carrots are
good for your heart.

Where was **hot chocolate** originally invented?

#77

a. ancient Egypt

b. ancient Mexico

c. ancient Middle East

ancient Mexico

THE PEOPLE OF THE ANCIENT OLMEC CIVILIZATION LIVED ABOUT 4,000 YEARS AGO IN WHAT IS NOW SOUTHERN MEXICO. They were the first people known to have used cacao beans to make something drinkable. The ancient Aztec and Maya civilizations, which came after, used cacao beans, too. **The first chocolate drinks were made of cacao beans but were unsweetened,** so the taste was bitter, not sweet as we usually think of hot chocolate. The Maya drank chocolate drinks with meals and during celebrations. **And the Aztec believed that drinking chocolate gave the drinker a special strength.**

NOW YOU KNOW!
Sugar was added to hot chocolate in the early 1700s, about 200 years after cacao beans were brought to Europe.

An Aztec woman making hot chocolate

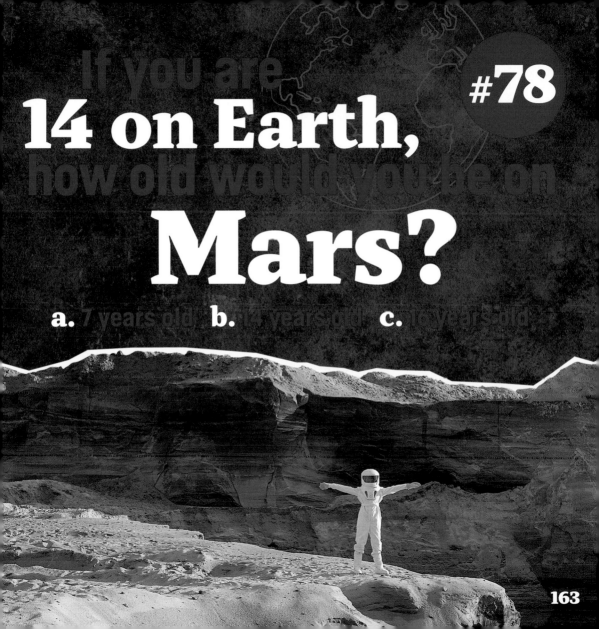

If you are

14 on Earth, how old would you be on Mars?

a. 7 years old   b. 14 years old   c. 16 years old

 ANSWER: **a**

7 years old

ON EARTH, THE LENGTH OF ONE DAY IS 24 HOURS. That's about how long it takes for our planet to make one complete rotation on its axis. The length of a Martian day is 24.6 hours, almost the same as Earth's. But the length of a Martian *year* is vastly different. **A year is measured by the amount of time it takes for a planet to complete one orbit around the sun.** It takes Earth 365 days to go once around the sun, which is one Earth year. **But because Mars is farther away from the sun, one orbit takes almost twice as long: 687 Earth days.** Because one year takes so long, your age on Mars would be about half of what it is on Earth.

Instant Genius

If you want to know your age on Mars, divide your Earth age by 1.88.

13 days old

WHEN IT COMES TO POLICE WORK, BLOODHOUNDS MAKE PARTICULARLY GOOD DETECTIVES. This is because bloodhounds have extraordinarily sensitive snouts: Researchers estimate that **their sense of smell is at least 10,000 times stronger than a human's.** When a bloodhound sniffs a piece of clothing, air rushes through the dog's nose. **Once a bloodhound has locked in on the scent, it can follow the scent's trail.** These dogs have such a strong sense of smell that they can track a scent that's almost 13 days old.

NOW YOU KNOW!
Bloodhounds have large, droopy ears that help prevent scents from being blown away by the wind while the dog is sniffing the ground.

Instant Genius
Bloodhounds were first trained 1,000 years ago in medieval times by monks.

Where is the biggest house in the world located?

a. Hollywood, U.S.A.

b. London, England

c. Mumbai, India

Mumbai, India

Instant Genius

Antilia has a staff of 600 people.

WITH 400,000 SQUARE FEET (37,160 SQ M) OF LIVING SPACE, A MEGA MANSION IN MUMBAI, INDIA, IS THE LARGEST HOUSE IN THE WORLD. Named Antilia, the house has 27 floors that are each two stories high. **It also contains a ballroom, guest suites, a theater that seats 50 people,** and a multistory garage with space for 168 cars! In case you prefer to arrive by air, **there are three helicopter pads on the roof.** There's also a spa, terraced gardens, and a temple, and a lobby with nine elevators. Earthquake? No problem. Antilia can survive an earthquake of 8 on the Richter scale.

NOW YOU KNOW!

Antilia is the second most expensive home in the world after Buckingham Palace, home to England's Queen Elizabeth.

True or False:

Pigeons can do **math.**

#81

Hey, look at me!

Instant Genius

Pigeons can recognize themselves in a mirror.

ANSWER: **True**

COMMON PIGEONS ARE VERY CLEVER ANIMALS. With training, not only are they intelligent enough to identify each letter of the alphabet, they can even count and do math! **In a recent study, researchers first trained them to identify screens showing different numbers of objects.** Once they understood the concept, the pigeons could then successfully peck the screens, putting the number of objects in order from lowest to highest. **Some primates, such as chimpanzees, can do this, too.**

#82

True or False:

When in space, astronauts' urine gets recycled into clean drinking water.

ANSWER: True

THE INTERNATIONAL SPACE STATION (ISS) USES A SPECIAL RECYCLING SYSTEM THAT MAKES CLEAN, DRINKABLE WATER from icky stuff like urine, sweat, wastewater, and other liquids on the ISS. This is really important because **having a constant water supply is one of the biggest challenges of space travel.** If astronauts are able to produce clean water without worrying about it running out, they may one day be able to travel in space for longer periods of time. **Maybe one day they might even reach Mars.**

life in the ISS

True or False:

Alligators

have been found living in the

sewers

of New York City.

If you can make it there . . .

#83

AN URBAN LEGEND IS A STRANGE STORY THAT MAY HAVE HAD SOME TRUTH TO IT BUT IS MOSTLY MADE-UP. For more than a century, tales of alligators living in New York City sewers were **thought to be an urban legend.** But some are actually true! Though it is illegal in New York State to buy, sell, or own alligators without a permit, **the city rescues several alligators— usually former illegal pets—every year.** Reports of these rescues go back more than 100 years.

Sculpture in New York City

Who named the planet Pluto?

#84

a. President Herbert Hoover

b. Neil Armstrong

c. Venetia Burney

175

Lowell Observatory

ANSWER: C

Venetia Burney

IN 1930, AN ASTRONOMER AT LOWELL OBSERVATORY IN ARIZONA, U.S.A., DECLARED HE HAD DISCOVERED THE NINTH PLANET IN OUR SOLAR SYSTEM. Its name was later suggested by Venetia Burney, **an 11-year-old girl from Oxford, England.** She thought Pluto, the name of the Roman god of the underworld, would be a fitting name. Officials at the observatory must have agreed! **In 2006, however, Pluto was reclassified as a dwarf planet.** Why? There are three qualifications to be considered a planet: an object must orbit the sun; it must be big enough that its gravity can pull it into a sphere shape; **it must be big enough that its gravity removes any other objects in its orbit.** Pluto did not meet the last qualification because it is in an area called the Kuiper Belt, an area where icy objects live.

NOW YOU KNOW!

One year on Pluto is about 248 Earth years. This means that since it was discovered in 1930, it hasn't even made one orbit around the sun!

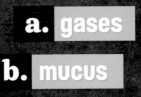

#85

Your stomach would **digest itself** if it didn't contain what substance?

a. gases

b. mucus

c. water

177

ANSWER: **b**

MUCUS

Instant Genius

A person's stomach acid is so strong it can dissolve metal!

YOUR STOMACH IS AN AMAZING ORGAN. A pouch shaped kind of like a large comma, **it produces around a gallon (roughly 3 to 4 L) of gastric juices a day.** These juices break down food, absorb nutrients, and kill bacteria. **The main digestive juice, known as hydrochloric acid, breaks down food to a pulp** so the body can absorb the nutrients. The stomach wall is made up of several layers of sticky mucus membrane, connective tissue with blood vessels, nerves, and muscle fibers. The mucus covers the stomach wall like a shield. **Without it, stomach acids would make painful holes.**

All cats are born with what  color eyes?

a. blue eyes **b.** brown eyes **c.** different-colored eyes, depending on the cat

ANSWER: **a**

blue eyes

A KITTEN'S EYELIDS ARE SEALED CLOSED TO PROTECT ITS EYES WHILE IT'S BEING BORN. About 10 days later, the kitten will open its lids to reveal bluish eyes. Its eye color will change as the kitten gets older and the cells in the kitten's body start making melanin, a pigment that determines color. **Cats with brown eyes have a large amount of melanin in the iris, the colored area around the eye's pupil.** Cats with blue eyes have much less of this pigment. Cats' eye colors can include yellow, green, brown, or blue. **If your kitten still has blue eyes at eight weeks of age, chances are good that its eyes will stay blue.**

NOW YOU KNOW!
Some animals have a different color in each eye. This is called heterochromia.

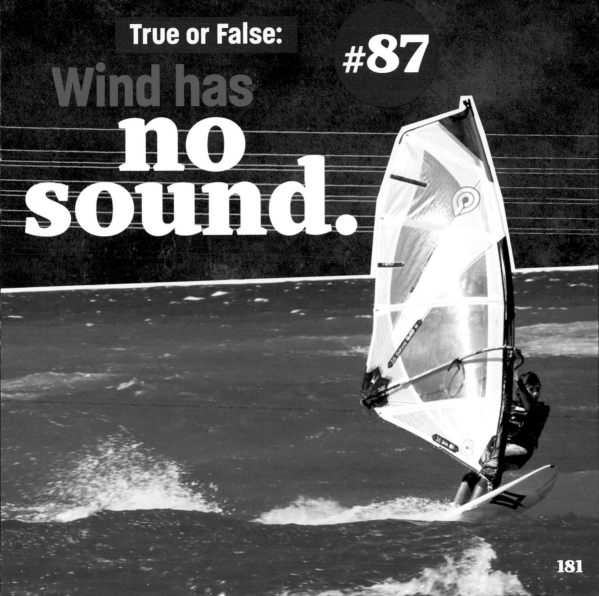

True or False: #87

Wind has **no sound.**

181

ANSWER: **True**

WIND IS AIR MOVING OVER EARTH, AND IT IS SILENT UNTIL IT COMES INTO CONTACT WITH SOMETHING ELSE. The whooshing you hear on a windy day is actually **the friction of the air moving against trees, buildings, or anything else is in its path.** Changes in air pressure—the weight of air pressing down on Earth—causes wind. **The strongest winds in our solar system occur on the planets Neptune and Saturn.**

Neptune

Saturn

How many hairs do you **lose** each day?

#88

 **a.** about 10 to 20

 **b.** about 50 to 100

 **c.** about 1,000

A hair follicle under a microscope

ANSWER: C

about 1,000

HUMANS ARE BORN WITH AROUND 5 MILLION HAIR FOLLICLES ALL OVER OUR BODIES, AND WE LOSE ABOUT 1,000 HAIRS EACH DAY. The shape of the follicle (a small pouch in the skin where hair grows out) determines whether hair is curly, wavy, or straight. Hair helps protect us from the elements by covering our skin. Hair also lets us know when something brushes by. On average, human hair grows about 6 inches (15 cm) a year, or about half an inch (1.3 cm) per month.

Instant Genius

About 90 percent of people have brown or black hair.

#89

True or False:

Grasshoppers
use color to
protect themselves.

185

ANSWER: **True**

SOME ANIMALS ARE BRIGHTLY COLORED TO COMMUNICATE THAT THEY ARE POISONOUS—EVEN WHEN THEY AREN'T. They use color as a defense mechanism to stop a potential predator from attacking. **The rainbow grasshopper, which lives in the United States, Canada, and northern Mexico,** relies on this "warning coloration" for protection. **It isn't poisonous, but its bright colors signal to predators to stay away.**

How did
Charles Darwin
change the world?

a. He invented the camera.

b. He developed the theory of natural selection.

c. He discovered the Galápagos Islands.

He developed the theory of natural selection.

CHARLES DARWIN WAS AN ENGLISH SCIENTIST WHO STUDIED NATURE. He formulated a theory of evolution by natural selection. Darwin explained that all living things struggle to survive, but when they do, the traits that made survival possible get passed down from generation to generation. This means that **members of a species that are able to adapt are more likely to survive and pass down a stronger trait to their offspring.** Over time, the trait becomes more common in that species. For example, about 8,000 years ago, sand from the Rocky Mountains blew east to what is now Nebraska. The mice that lived there were a darker brown color. **Over time, some mice developed a lighter brown fur to blend in with the color of the new sand.** This adaptation allowed those mice to stay hidden and survive in their new environment. Over time, mice with darker fur died out because they were easily seen by predators.

#91

True or False:

If your cat stares at you, it could be a sign of affection.

189

ANSWER: **True**

CATS STARE AT THEIR OWNERS FOR DIFFERENT REASONS. Instinct may have something to do with this habit. Before they were domesticated, **cats had to keep watch over their environment for signs of danger.** The instinct to stare remains today, even though most cats don't have to hunt for their food anymore. Since cats are naturally curious, **your cat will be interested in what you're doing, even if it's just homework.** Staring can also be a form of communication. For example, a long, unblinking look may be **your cat's way of communicating that it trusts you, which is how it shows affection.**

What is the oldest material ever found on Earth?

a. stardust   **b.** gold   **c.** silver

ANSWER: **a**

stardust

THE OLDEST STUFF EVER FOUND ON EARTH IS STARDUST.
Scientists discovered it in a meteorite that hit our planet more than 50 years ago. When studying it, they discovered that **part of the stardust was 7 billion years old—older than the sun!** Scientists believe the dust shot out from dying stars and that some of it landed on an asteroid. **A chunk of that asteroid broke off and became a meteoroid.** Once a meteoroid enters Earth's atmosphere, it becomes a meteor. If that meteor doesn't burn up, it becomes a meteorite. That's what happened with this chunk of rock—**it headed to Earth, made it through the atmosphere, and landed in Australia in 1969.**

Instant Genius

Earth's sun is 4.6 billion years old.

A fragment of the meteorite shown next to a sample of its material in a test tube, used for analysis of its chemical makeup

ANSWER: True

AN OPPOSABLE THUMB CAN ROTATE ON THE HAND TO TOUCH THE OTHER FINGERS. Humans have opposable thumbs and **so do chimpanzees, koalas, and bats, among others.** There are flexible bones in a bat's wings that work like fingers. This allows bats to have a full range of movement, which makes them agile flyers. A bat's thumbs sit along the front edge of its wings; their size depends on the species. For instance, **bat species whose roosting (coming together to sleep) and feeding behavior involve crawling have stronger thumbs.**

Koala

What do the minerals alexandrite and benitoite have in common?

#94

a. They are both part of a healthy diet.

b. They are both rare gemstones.

c. They are both retired crayon colors.

Benitoite

Alexandrite

ANSWER: b

They are both rare gemstones.

DIAMONDS, RUBIES, SAPPHIRES, AND EMERALDS ARE SOME OF THE MOST POPULAR GEMSTONES, BUT THERE ARE ACTUALLY MORE THAN 200 VARIETIES OF GEMS. Some are so rare that they are more valuable than diamonds! **Benitoite has a deep-blue color and glows under UV light.** It was discovered in California in 1906 and became the state's official gemstone in 1985. Because it's so rare, a well-cut, two-carat benitoite stone can cost more than $20,000. **Alexandrite, which was discovered in Russia in 1830, also changes color.** This stone looks blue-green in sunlight and reddish-purple under indoor light.

NOW YOU KNOW!
The olive-green-colored stone peridot has been found in meteorites that have landed on Earth.

Instant Genius
Diamonds are one of the hardest materials on Earth.

Which land mammal is the fastest eater?

a. the star-nosed mole

b. the capybara

c. the anteater

Time me!

the star-nosed mole

A STAR-NOSED MOLE CAN FIND AND CATCH A MEAL IN A FRACTION OF A SECOND, which is faster than any other mammal on land. **Its nose is a hairless organ with 22 pink tentacles in the shape of a star.** With more than 100,000 tiny sensors packed into a space smaller than a dime, this nose is the most touch-sensitive known organ in the animal world. **The nearly blind, hamster-size rodent lives in wet, marshy areas of eastern North America,** using its supersensitive snout in place of eyesight to identify and eat bugs in record time.

Instant Genius

Star-nosed moles can also detect odors underwater, another place they search for prey.

What is the human body's largest organ?

a. the brain

b. the heart

c. neither the brain nor the heart

ANSWER: C

neither the brain nor the heart

THE SKIN IS THE BODY'S LARGEST ORGAN. Like a shield, it protects us from the elements, helps regulate our body temperature, and allows us to **feel heat, cold, and other sensations through touch.** There are nearly 20 million skin cells on each inch of the human body, and it sheds 30,000 to 40,000 of them every day. **Within a month, you will have shed your entire skin and regrown a new one.** Where does all that skin go? It becomes dust.

About how many species of insects exist on Earth?

#97

a. about 5.5 million

b. about 1.5 million

c. about 2.5 million

ANSWER: a

about 5.5 million

THERE ARE MORE SPECIES OF INSECTS ON EARTH THAN OF ANY OTHER ANIMAL SPECIES. Scientists estimate that there are at least 5.5 million different kinds of insects—**and probably even more than that.** Insects live in almost every kind of habitat, including deserts and mountains. **Many also call the rain forest home, where butterflies, bees, and dragonflies fly among the lush trees.** Because the tree cover is so thick in a rain forest, little sunlight gets to the forest floor. Plants can't survive down there, but there is nutritious soil for ants and beetles and many other creepy-crawlies that scamper about.

Which is the only sport ever to be played on the **moon?**

a. tennis

b. golf

c. soccer

ASTRONAUT ALAN SHEPARD WAS THE FIRST AMERICAN IN SPACE. He is also one of only a dozen people to have walked on the moon. **In 1971, Shepard was commander of Apollo 14,** the third Apollo mission to land on the moon. While there, the astronauts took photographs, collected soil samples, and conducted other research. But it was not all work and no play. **Shepard put together a makeshift golf club, and he hit two golf balls while on the moon.**

Instant Genius

Apollo 14 astronauts brought back 94 pounds (43 kg) of moon rocks and soil.

NOW YOU KNOW!

Since the moon has no atmosphere and very little gravity, a golf ball can travel a lot farther when hit there than it can on Earth.

99

True or False:

No two zebras have the same pattern of **stripes.**

ANSWER: **True**

ZEBRAS SPORT THE MOST RECOGNIZABLE COAT IN THE ANIMAL KINGDOM. But did you know that each zebra's stripes are unique, like a human's fingerprints? **Each species has its own pattern, and, within those patterns, no two markings are exactly alike.** Scientists think that a zebra's pattern of stripes serves several purposes: as camouflage to confuse predators as they move across the savanna, as a way for zebras to identify one another, and to help keep disease-carrying flies from biting them. **All three species of zebra live in Africa.**

Instant Genius

A rare polka-dotted zebra was once *spotted* in Kenya.

In Japan, there are **more pets** than children.

#100

ANSWER: True

OVER THE PAST FEW DECADES, THE NUMBER OF REGISTERED PET DOGS AND CATS IN JAPAN HAS CLIMBED TO MORE THAN 19 MILLION. This outnumbers the total number of children under the age of 15, which is 15 million. **In Japan, dogs and cats are considered members of the family.** Since most people in Japan live in smaller spaces, such as apartments, small dog breeds, including chihuahuas, toy poodles, and miniature dachshunds, are popular. **And cats have become even more popular than dogs.**

Instant Genius

Japan's Aoshima Island, known as "cat island," is home to more felines than people.

How long have **sea turtles** lived on Earth?

a. more than 1 million years

b. more than 10 million years

c. more than 100 million years

ANSWER: C

more than 100 million years

Fossil of a prehistoric turtle

SEA TURTLES HAVE BEEN ON EARTH FOR ABOUT 110 MILLION YEARS. In fact, they lived at the same times as dinosaurs! There are seven species of sea turtle. **The largest are leatherbacks, which weigh as much as 2,000 pounds (907 kg) and can be up to 9 feet (2.7 m) long.** Sea turtles live in warm ocean waters all over the world, swimming thousands of miles each year. When it's time to lay her eggs, **a female sea turtle will swim back to the same beach where she hatched.**

Spot the 7 Random Differences:

Turn to page 215 for the answers!

Index

Page numbers in *italic* refer to images.

Photo Credits

The publishers would like to thank the following for the use of their images. While every effort has been made to credit images, the publishers will be pleased to correct any errors or omissions in future editions of the book.

t = top; b = bottom; l = left; r = right; c = center

123rf.com: pp. 190, 191(r).

Alamy: pp. 12(tr), 24, 32(l), 44(r), 59, 60(t), 76(t), 83, 86(br), 89, 94(t), 108(t), 119, 123(bl,bc), 128(t), 138(tr), 168(r), 175(br), 196(tl), 197(cl), 206(br).

Dreamstime: pp. 1, 2(tl,br), 5(tr), 6(cl,br), 7(t,cr), 8, 9(tr,br), 11, 13(l,c,br), 14(t,cr), 15(bl,bc,cr), 16(t), 17(tr,br), 18(br), 19, 20, 22(cr), 25, 27, 28, 29, 30(t,br), 31, 36(br), 37, 38(tl,bl,br), 39, 40(bl,r), 41, 42(t,br), 44(bc), 45, 47, 48(br), 49, 50(t,br), 51, 52(t,br), 53, 57 (cl,br), 60(bl), 61, 62(t,br), 63, 65, 66, 67, 69, 71, 72(l,br), 73, 74(bc), 77, 78, 79, 82(br), 84(bl,r), 85, 86(t), 87, 88(t), 90(br), 91, 92(tl,cr), 93(l,c,r), 94(cr), 95(l,cr,br), 96(br), 97, 98(t,br), 99(cr,br), 101(l,bc,br), 102(br), 103, 104(l), 105, 106(t,br), 108(br), 111, 112, 114(t), 115, 116(l,br), 117, 118(t,bl), 120(tr,br), 121, 122(t,br), 123(br), 125, 127, 128(br), 129, 130, 131, 132(br), 133(br), 134(bl), 136(bl), 137, 138(bl), 139, 140(bl,r), 141(l,c,r), 142, 143, 144, 146, 147, 149, 150(tl,tr,br), 151, 152, 153, 154, 155, 156(b), 157, 158(cr), 159, 160, 161(l,c,r), 162(bl,r), 163, 164(t), 165, 166(bl,r), 167(l,c,r), 168(bcl), 169, 170(t,br), 171, 173, 174(tr,b), 176(tl), 177, 178, 180(t,br), 181, 182(t), 183, 184(t,br), 185, 186, 187, 188, 189, 191(c), 193, 194(t,br), 195(l,c,r), 196(tr,cr), 197(bl,cr), 199(l,r), 200(t,br), 203(l,c,r), 205, 206(t), 207, 208(tl,cr), 209, 210(bl), 211(t,b), 215.

©Festo SE & Co. KG, all rights reserved: p. 56(br).

Getty Images: pp. 23, 35, 36(l), 81, 82(t), 90(t), 124.

iStockphoto: pp. 16(br), 18(l), 26, 46, 57(bl), 58, 64, 96(t), 99(l), 113, 114(br), 132(t), 133(tc,cl), 145, 179, 201.

Library of Congress: pp. 43, 175(bl).

NASA (National Aeronautics and Space Administration): pp. 4, 33, 34, 68, 109, 110, 120(tl), 126, 135, 136(t), 148, 156(tr), 158(b), 164(bl), 172(t,br), 175(bc), 176(cr), 182(bc,br), 191(l), 192(main photo), 204(main photo,tr).

Nature Picture Library: pp. 5(c), 10, 12(b), 21, 22(t), 32(tr), 54, 70, 75, 76(br), 100(bl,r), 198, 202, 210(t).

NOAA (National Oceanic and Atmospheric Administration) National Environmental Satellite, Data, and Information Service (NESDIS): p. 102(t).

Professor Ingo Rechenberg: pp. 55, 56(t).

Science Photo Library: pp. 104(br), 134(br).

Shutterstock: p. 88(br).

US Department of Energy: p. 192(bc).

Wikimedia Commons: pp. 48(main photo: Dan/CC BY 2.0), 74(r), 80(main photo,br), 107.

Credits

Text and cover design copyright © 2022 by
Penguin Random House LLC

All rights reserved. Published in the United States by Random House
Children's Books, a division of Penguin Random House LLC, New York.

Random House and the colophon are registered trademarks of
Penguin Random House LLC.

Visit us on the Web! **rhcbooks.com**

Educators and librarians, for a variety of teaching tools, visit us
at **RHTeachersLibrarians.com**

Library of Congress Cataloging-in-Publication Data is available
upon request.
ISBN 978-0-593-45031-4 (trade)
ISBN 978-0-593-45037-6 (lib. bdg.)
ISBN 978-0-593-51612-6 (ebook)

COVER PHOTO CREDITS:
Front Cover Photo: Shutterstock.
Back Cover Photo: Dreamstime.

MANUFACTURED IN ITALY
10 9 8 7 6 5 4 3 2 1
First Edition

Produced by Fun Factory Press, LLC, in association with
Potomac Global Media, LLC.

The publisher would like to thank the following people for their
contributions to this book: Melina Gerosa Bellows, President,
Fun Factory Press, and Series Creator and Author; Priyanka
Lamichhane, Editor and Project Manager; Chad Tomlinson, Art
Director; Jen Agresta, Copy Editor; Michelle Harris, Fact-checker;
Potomac Global Media: Kevin Mulroy, Publisher; Barbara Brownell
Grogan, Editor-in-Chief; Thomas Keenes, Designer; Susannah
Jayes and Ellen Dupont, Picture Researchers; Jane Sunderland,
Proofreader